Right to Peaceful Assembly

European Court of Human Rights

France • Italy • Portugal• Spain • Sweden
United Kingdom • United States

October 2014

The Law Library of Congress, Global Legal Research Center
(202) 707-6462 (phone) • (866) 550-0442 (fax) • law@loc.gov • http://www.law.gov

Contents

Summary

Freedom of peaceful assembly is a recognized right under international human rights law. This report provides a comparative review of one aspect of this right: whether advance notification or authorization is required for an assembly to take place under the law of France, Italy, Portugal, Spain, Sweden, the United Kingdom, and the United States. The report also reviews the relevant case law of the European Court of Human Rights (ECHR).

Article 11 of the European Convention on Human Rights and Fundamental Freedoms protects the right to peacefully assemble, but that right is not absolute; state authorities are given "a margin of appreciation" and may impose certain restrictions on the exercise of this right, provided that such limitations are (a) prescribed by law; (b) necessary in a democratic society; and (c) in the interests of national security or public safety, for the prevention of disorder or crime, for the protection of health or morals, or for the protection of the rights and freedoms of others. Similarly, in the United States, restrictions related to time, manner, and place imposed by government authorities can be justified as long as they are content-neutral, narrowly tailored to serve significant government interests, and leave other lines of communication open.

While Article 11 does not require organizers to submit advance notification to state authorities or request authorization, all of the countries surveyed require advance notification, except Sweden, which requires either authorization or notification depending on the type of assembly, and the United States, where the Supreme Court has held that it is permissible under the US Constitution for a government to require a permit to hold a peaceful assembly. The Venice Commission of the Council of Europe recommends that states that require authorization opt for notification as a less burdensome requirement.

As far as how far in advance notification is required to be provided to state authorities, Portugal requires a minimum of two days, France and Italy require three days, the United Kingdom requires six days, and Sweden requires seven days.

The ECHR, which is the final arbiter of human rights violations in the forty-seven Member States of the Council of Europe, has upheld the right to peaceful assembly in many cases. It has found that a mere lack of notification, without any misconduct by participants, does not justify the dispersal of a peaceful assembly, and that any governmental restrictions must meet the three criteria stated above. The ECHR has also held that the right to peacefully assemble for religious ceremonies or worship should be construed in light of the right to freedom of religion, which is guaranteed under article 9 of the European Convention on Human Rights.

European Court of Human Rights

Theresa Papademetriou
Senior Foreign Law Specialist

I. Introduction

The European Convention on Human Rights and Fundamental Freedoms and its protocols (the European Convention on Human Rights) is an international treaty adopted by the Council of Europe to protect and safeguard the rights and freedoms of individuals living within the jurisdiction of the forty-seven Member States of the Council of Europe who have ratified the Convention.[1] In 1959, the European Convention on Human Rights established a system composed of the European Commission of Human Rights, the European Court of Human Rights, and the Committee of Ministers to hear allegations of violations of human rights and enforce compliance by the states parties.[2] In 1998, Protocol No. 11 abolished the European Commission and established the European Court of Human Rights as the only judicial organ to adjudicate cases instituted before it by individuals, nongovernmental organizations, or group of victims.[3]

II. Right to Peaceful Assembly

The right to peaceful assembly is established in article 11 of the European Convention on Human Rights.[4] States parties may impose certain limitations on the exercise of this right. However, such restrictions must be (a) prescribed by law; (b) necessary in a democratic society; and (c) in the interests of national security or public safety, for the prevention of disorder or crime, for the protection of health or morals, or for the protection of the rights and freedoms of others.[5] Article 11 of the European Convention not only protects an individual's right to peaceful assembly, but also imposes a positive obligation on state authorities to facilitate the exercise of this right and enable assemblies to take place peacefully.[6]

---

[1] European Convention on the Protection of Human Rights and Fundamental Freedoms, Sept. 3, 1953, 213 U.N.T.S. 222, *as amended*, http://www.echr.coe.int/documents/convention_eng.pdf.

[2] 50 YEARS OF ACTIVITY: THE EUROPEAN COURT OF HUMAN RIGHTS: SOME FACTS AND FIGURES 3, http://www.echr.coe.int/Documents/Facts_Figures_1959_2009_ENG.pdf (last visited Oct. 1, 2014).

[3] Protocol No. 11 to the Convention for the Protection of Human Rights and Fundamental Freedoms, Restructuring the Control Machinery Established Thereby, May 11, 1994, entered into force Nov. 1, 1998, http://conventions.coe.int/Treaty/en/Treaties/Html/155.htm.

[4] European Convention on the Protection of Human Rights, *supra* note 1, art. 11(1).

[5] *Id.* art. 1(2).

[6] JIM MURDOCH & RALPH ROCHE, THE EUROPEAN CONVENTION ON HUMAN RIGHTS AND POLICING 103 (Dec. 2013), *available at* http://www.coe.int/t/dghl/cooperation/capacitybuilding/Source/documentation/EuropeanConventionHandbookForPolice.pdf.

III. Advance Notification and Authorization of Assemblies

In general, international human rights law and specifically article 11 of the European Convention do not require that advance notification of a forthcoming assembly be given.[7] However, contracting states may request prior notification in order to take the necessary measures to protect public order and the rights and freedoms of others.[8] Thus, the purpose of providing prior notification is to indicate the intent of the organizers involved; it must not amount to permission.[9] The now defunct European Commission on Human Rights stated in *Rassemblement Jurassien Unité Jurassienne v. Switzerland* that "[s]uch a procedure is in keeping with the requirements of Article 11(1) [of the Convention], if only in order that the authorities may be in a position to ensure the peaceful nature of the meeting, and accordingly does not as such constitute interference with the exercise of the right."[10]

The Guidelines on Freedom of Peaceful Assembly prepared by the Venice Commission of the Council of Europe and the Office for Democratic Institutions and Human Rights (ODIHR) of the Organization on Security and Co-operation in Europe (OSCE) provide that states may require notification when large assemblies are to take place or not require notification in the case of certain assemblies.[11] The Guidelines cite as an example the laws of Moldova and Poland, which do not require notification for small assemblies.[12]

The Guidelines do not endorse a permit requirement because such a requirement is more "prone to abuse than notification,"[13] and recommend that countries that require permission to hold assemblies amend their domestic legislation to require only notification.[14] The Guidelines also cite the Constitutional Court of Georgia, which declared part of a law requiring a permit procedure unconstitutional.[15]

There are no rules regarding how far in advance notification should be provided by organizers to state authorities. The Venice Commission states that a few days should be sufficient to allow state authorities to take any necessary precautions and also to allow organizers to challenge in

---

[7] OSCE/ODIHR, VENICE COMMISSION GUIDELINES ON FREEDOM OF PEACEFUL ASSEMBLY (GUIDELINES) paras. 113–117 (2d ed. July 9, 2010), http://www.venice.coe.int/webforms/documents/ default.aspx?pdffile=CDL-AD%282010%29020-e. The Guidelines and Explanatory Notes are based on international and regional treaties and state practices as derived from national court decisions.

[8] *Id.*

[9] *Id.* paras. 118–121.

[10] *Id.* para. 114 (quoting Rassemblement Jurassien Unité Jurassienne v. Switzerland (Eur. Comm'n H.R. 1979) at 119).

[11] *Id.*

[12] *Id.*

[13] *Id.* para. 118.

[14] *Id.* para. 119.

[15] GUIDELINES, *supra* note 7, at 56 n.182.

court an official negative response. The Commission also states that if a law specifies certain limits, these should only be indicative.[16]

IV. European Court of Human Rights

The European Court of Human Rights (ECHR) has produced a rich body of case law on the right to peaceful assembly. With regard to notification requirements, the ECHR reiterated in the case of *Eva Molnar v. Hungary* that

> a prior notification requirement would not normally encroach upon the essence of that right. It is not contrary to the spirit of Article 11 [of the Convention] if, for reasons of public order and national security, *a priori*, a High Contracting Party requires that the holding of meetings be subject to authorisation.[17]

The ECHR went on to say that the mere absence of prior notification can never serve as a legitimate basis for crowd dispersal; that prior notification serves the goal of reconciling the right to peaceful assembly with that of preventing disorder and crime; and that in order to balance these conflicting interests,

> the institution of preliminary administrative procedures is common practice in Member States when a public demonstration is to be organized. In the Court's view, such requirements do not, as such, run counter to the principles embodied in Article 11 of the Convention, as long as they do not represent a hidden obstacle to the freedom of peaceful assembly protected by the Convention.[18]

In the case of *Bukta and Others v. Hungary*, the ECHR found that Hungary had violated article 11 of the European Convention because the police had dispersed a peaceful assembly on the basis that it was held without prior notification.[19] Although the police were acting on the basis of Hungary's Right of Assembly Act 1989, which requires that the police be informed of an assembly at least three days in advance and gives the police the authority to disband an assembly that takes place without prior notification,[20] the ECHR held that a decision to dispel a peaceful assembly solely because of the failure of the organizers to comply with a notice requirement, without any illegal conduct by the participants, is a disproportionate restriction on peaceful assembly.[21]

---

[16] *Id.* para. 116.

[17] Éva Molnár v. Hungary, App. No. 10346/05 Final, Eur. Ct. H.R. (Jan. 7, 2009), http://hudoc.echr.coe.int/ sites/eng/pages/search.aspx?i=001-88775 (citing Nurettin Aldemir and Others v. Turkey, App. Nos. 32124/02, 32126/02, 32129/02, 32132/02, 32133/02, 32137/02 and 32138/02 (joined), § 42, Eur. Ct. H.R. (Dec. 18, 2007)).

[18] *Id.* at 37.

[19] Bukta and Others v. Hungary, App. No. 25691/04 Final, Eur. Ct. H.R. (Oct. 17, 2007), http://hudoc.echr.coe.int/ sites/eng/pages/search.aspx?i=001-81728.

[20] *Id.* para. 19.

[21] *Id.* para. 36.

Concerning the right to assemble for religious ceremonies or worship, the ECHR held in the 2007 case of *Barankevich v. Russia*[22] that the right to peaceful assembly must be interpreted in the light of article 9 of the European Convention, which guarantees freedom of religion.[23] In this case, the town authorities had refused, on the basis of a 1988 decree applicable at that time, to permit a minority religion (Christ's Grace Church of Evangelical Christians) to hold a religious service in a public park on the grounds that the service would provoke public disorder among the majority of residents, who practiced other religions.[24] The government argued that the imposed ban had been reviewed by domestic courts, which had upheld the decision of the town authorities.[25] The ECHR "welcomed" the fact that Russia had amended its law on public assemblies in 2004 to replace the requirement of prior authorization with simple notification of an intended assembly.[26] However, the ECHR stated that there was no justification for interfering with the rights of the followers of a religion merely because they were a minority group.[27] The Court also noted that there was no indication that those participating in the service would incite or resort to violence, nor any indication that the local authorities had considered adopting measures "necessary for neutralizing the threat" of a violent counter-demonstration and allowing the assembly to take place peacefully; instead they had "den[ied] the applicant the possibility of exercising his rights to freedom of religion and assembly."[28] Consequently, the ECHR found against Russia because the prohibition did not meet the test of being "necessary in a democratic society."[29]

---

[22]Barankevich v. Russia Final, App. No. 10519/03 Final, Eur. Ct. H.R. (Oct. 26, 2007), http://hudoc.echr.coe.int/sites/eng/pages/search.aspx?i=001-81950.

[23] *Id.* para. 35.

[24] *Id.* paras. 28–29.

[25] *Id.* para. 22.

[26] *Id.* para. 28.

[27] *Id.* para. 31.

[28] *Id.* paras. 32–33.

[29] *Id.* para. 35.

France

Nicolas Boring
Foreign Law Specialist

I. Right to Peaceably Assemble and Notification Requirement

Whereas the preamble of the French Constitution protects the right to strike,[1] there is no explicit protection of the right to peaceably assemble. The right to peaceably assemble can be inferred, however, from the 1789 Declaration of the Rights of Man and of the Citizen, which is incorporated into the current French Constitution. Article 10 of the Declaration states that "no one should be bothered for his opinions, even religious ones, so long as their manifestation does not disturb the public order established by Law."[2] Furthermore, the right to peaceably assemble is guaranteed by the European Convention on Human Rights, to which France is a party.[3]

Since 1935, the right to assemble in a public space has been contingent on prior notification.[4] Notification must be given to the local prefecture or to the town hall (*mairie*) of the town(s) where the demonstration or assembly is supposed to take place, at least three days, and no more than fifteen days, before the date of the demonstration or assembly.[5]

II. Authority to Prohibit Demonstrations

The authorities (the prefect or the mayor) may prohibit a demonstration if they believe that it would disturb public order.[6] Peaceful demonstrations must generally be allowed. If a demonstration is prohibited, the organizers may challenge the decision before an administrative

---

[1] CONSTITUTION DU 4 OCTOBRE 1958 [CONSTITUTION OF OCTOBER 4, 1958], Article Préambule [Preamble Article], http://www.legifrance.gouv fr/affichTexte.do?cidTexte=LEGITEXT000006071194, *referring to* CONSTITUTION DU 27 OCTOBRE 1946 [CONSTITUTION OF OCTOBER 27, 1946], Article Préambule [Preamble Article], http://www.legi france.gouv fr/affichTexte.do;jsessionid=358011F10FB952719BF7115C8D25B404.tpdjo17v 1?cidTexte=LEGITE XT000006071193&dateTexte=&categorieLien=cid.

[2] *Id., referring to* DÉCLARATION DES DROITS DE L'HOMME ET DU CITOYEN DE 1789 [DECLARATION OF THE RIGHTS OF MAN AND OF THE CITIZEN OF 1789], art. 10, http://www.legifrance.gouv fr/Droit-francais/Constitution/ Declaration-des-Droits-de-l-Homme-et-du-Citoyen-de-1789.

[3] See survey on the European Court of Human Rights.

[4] Décret-loi du 23 octobre 1935 portant réglementation des mesures relatives au renforcement du maintien de l'ordre public [Law-Decree of October 23, 1935, Establishing Regulations on Measures Related to the Reinforcement of Public Order] art. 1 (Oct. 23, 1935), http://www.legifrance.gouv.fr/affichTexte.do;jsessionid=CCB2BA530CFBA 7AE61800A4C7153C625.tpdjo17v 1?cidTexte=LEGITEXT000006071320&dateTexte=20120430. These provisions were codified into the CODE DE LA SÉCURITÉ INTÉRIEURE [INTERIOR SECURITY CODE] art. L211-1, http://www.legifrance.gouv fr/affichCode.do;jsessionid=CCB2BA530CFBA7AE61800A4C7153C625.tpdjo17v 1? cidTexte=LEGITEXT000025503132&dateTexte=20140923.

[5] CODE DE LA SÉCURITÉ INTÉRIEURE art. L211-2.

[6] *Id.* art. L211-4.

judge, who will verify whether such a prohibition is necessary to protect public order and security.[7]

III. Court Case on Peaceful Assembly

The Conseil d'Etat, France's highest court for administrative matters, recently found that a prefect's decision to prohibit a pro-Palestine demonstration in Paris was justified. The demonstration, scheduled for July 26, 2014, was prohibited by Paris's Prefect of Police based on fears that it would turn violent. These fears rested in large part on the fact that two previous demonstrations on the same issue, which took place on July 13 and July 19, 2014, gave rise to violent clashes and considerable destruction of property, in spite of the deployment of large numbers of police forces.[8]

---

[7] *Manifestations à caractère revendicatif* [*Protest Demonstrations*], PRÉFET DU NORD [PREFECT OF THE NORTH], LES SERVICES DE L'ETAT DANS LE NORD [SERVICES OF THE STATE IN THE NORTH] (Jan. 24, 2014), http://www.nord.gouv. fr/Demarches-administratives/Activites-et-professions-reglementees/Manifestations-a-caractere-revendicatif.

[8] C.E. Référé, July 26, 2014, No. 383091, *M. C. et autres* [*M. C. and Others*].

Italy

Dante Figueroa
Senior Legal Information Analyst

Pursuant to Part I of Italy's Political Constitution, citizens have a constitutional right to peaceful and unarmed assembly (*diritto di riunirsi pacificamente e senz'armi*).[1] The right to peaceful assembly is generally recognized as a human right in Italy and is protected by both international and domestic law.[2]

The Constitution makes a distinction between meetings held in private places, meetings held in places open to the public, and meetings in public places. For meetings held in private places and places open to the public (e.g., stadiums and theaters), no previous notice to the authorities is required.[3] In the original version of Royal Decree (R.D.) No. 773 of 1931, a private meeting was considered to be public when the number of persons attending or the meeting's scope or purpose gave it the character of a nonprivate meeting.[4] However, a decision of the Italian Constitutional Court in 1958 abrogated this provision.[5]

For meetings in public places, previous notice must be given to the authorities, who may forbid such meetings only for proven reasons of security and public safety.[6] In effect, under domestic law, the only conditions limiting the right to assembly are that gatherings must be peaceful and their participants must not carry weapons, as provided in the Constitution. A peaceful assembly is defined as one that does not "disturb the public order" (*turbi l'ordine pubblico*).[7] The Italian Constitution does not require permission to hold meetings in public places; because citizens are exercising a right guaranteed by the Constitution, prior notice suffices.[8]

---

[1] COSTITUZIONE DELLA REPUBBLICA ITALIANA [COST.] [CONSTITUTION OF THE ITALIAN REPUBLIC] art. 17, para. 1, available on the Senate of the Republic website, *at* https://www.senato.it/documenti/repository/istituzione/ costituzione.pdf, English version *available at* http://www.senato.it/documenti/repository/istituzione/costituzione inglese.pdf.

[2] LIVIO PALADIN, DIRITTO COSTITUZIONALE [CONSTITUTIONAL LAW] 640 (1998); *Libertà di riunione e associazione* [*Freedom of Assembly and Association*], HUMAN RIGHTS EDUCATION ASSOCIATES, http://www.hrea.org/index.php ?doc_id=407 (last visited Sept. 5, 2014).

[3] COST. art. 17, para. 2; *see also* Laura Mazzavillani, La Libertà di Riunione – Art. 17 Cost., http://www.mazzavillani.it/approfondimenti/ app_diritto13.htm (course materials; last visited Sept. 5, 2014).

[4] Regio Decreto 18 giugno 1931, n. 773, Testo unico delle leggi di pubblica sicurezza [Royal Decree [R.D.] No. 773 of June 18, 1931, Consolidated Public Safety Law] art. 18, para. 2, Supplement to GAZETTA UFFICIALE [G.U.] [OFFICIAL GAZETTE] No. 146, June 26, 1931, *available at* http://www.siulp.it/siulp/wp-content/risorse/2013/07/ tulps.pdf.

[5] Decision of the Italian Constitutional Court No. 27 of March 31, 1958, *cited in* ANGELO MATTIONI, IL CODICE COSTITUZIONALE [THE CONSTITUTIONAL CODE] 645 (2013).

[6] COST. art. 17, para. 3.

[7] *Libertà di riunione* [*Freedom of Assembly*], TRECCANI.IT, http://www.treccani.it/enciclopedia/liberta-di-riunione/ (translation by the author; last visited Sept. 5, 2014).

[8] *Id.*

The main statutory provisions implementing the constitutional right to peaceful assembly are contained in articles 18–24 of R.D. No. 773. These provisions, among other regulations, establish that the advance notice required by article 17 of the Constitution must be given to the *questore* (superintendent—a provincial authority in charge of public safety) at least three days prior to the day of the meeting.[9] Violation of the notice provisions is punishable by imprisonment and fines.[10] Based on considerations of public order, morality, and public health, the superintendent may prohibit the meeting, or establish the time and place of the meeting.[11]

The authorities may dissolve a meeting held in a public place or in a place open to the public if shouting or demonstrations erupt that are seditious, damaging to the prestige of the authorities, or threatening to the public order or the safety of citizens, or when crimes are committed during those demonstrations or gatherings.[12] The display of flags or emblems that are symbols of social subversion, rebellion, or contempt toward the state, the government, or the authorities are always considered seditious,[13] as are the display of *distintivi* (badges) of partisan associations.[14]

Public safety officers or, in their absence, officers or deputy officers of the police (*ufficiali di pubblica sicurezza o, in loro assenza, dagli ufficiali o dai sottufficiali dei carabinieri*) may request those assembled in unauthorized meetings to disperse.[15] If such a request is disobeyed, dissolution of the meeting may be ordered through three formal notices, each of them preceded by the sounding of a trumpet.[16] If those in attendance do not heed the order, the above-referenced officers may forcibly dissolve the meeting.[17] Resisting dispersal is punishable by arrest and a fine.[18]

The carrying of firearms and other weapons in public meetings without authorization from the authorities is prohibited.[19] Law No. 110 of April 18, 1975, lists a series of weapons that may not

---

[9] R.D. 773, art. 18, para. 1; Alessandro Amaolo, *Testo Unico di Pubblica Sicurezza: brevi riflessioni su alcuni profili* [*Consolidated Law on Public Security: Brief Reflections on Several Provisions*], ALTALEX (Oct. 7, 2013), http://www.altalex.com/index.php?idnot=64740.

[10] R.D. 773, art. 18, para. 3.

[11] *Id.* art. 18, para. 4; PALADIN, *supra* note 2, at 1.

[12] R.D. 773, art. 20.

[13] *Id.* art. 21, para. 1.

[14] *Id.* art. 21, para. 2.

[15] *Id.* art. 22.

[16] *Id.* art. 23.

[17] *Id.* art. 24, para. 1.

[18] *Id.* art. 24, para. 3.

[19] *Id.* art. 42.

be carried outside of one's own residence.[20] Holders of weapons permits are also forbidden from carrying weapons in public meetings.[21]

---

[20] Legge 18 aprile 1975, n. 110, Norme integrative della disciplina vigente per il controllo delle armi, delle munizioni e degli esplosivi [Law No. 110 of April 18, 1975, Additional Provisions Related to the Control of Arms, Ammunition and Explosives] art. 42, paras. 1 & 2, G.U. No. 105, Apr. 21, 1975, *available at* http://www.normattiva.it/uri-res/N2Ls?urn:nir:stato:legge:1975-04-18;110!vig.

[21] *Id.* art. 42, para. 4.

Portugal

Eduardo Soares
Senior Foreign Law Specialist

Article 45 of the Portuguese Constitution provides that citizens have the right to peaceful and unarmed assembly, even in public places, without prior authorization,[1] and recognizes every citizen's right to demonstrate (*direito de manifestação*).[2]

The right to assemble and the right to demonstrate are regulated by Decree-Law No. 406 of August 29, 1974, which reaffirms the following:

> Every citizen is guaranteed the free exercise of the right to peaceful assembly in public places that are open to the public and to individual parties, regardless of authorization, for purposes that are not contrary to the law, to moral standards, to the rights of natural or legal persons, and to order and public tranquility.[3] . . . Notwithstanding the right to criticize, meetings that are organized for the purpose of offending the honor and consideration that are due to governing bodies and the armed forces are prohibited.[4]
>
> . . .
>
> Persons or entities who wish to hold meetings, rallies, demonstrations, or parades in public places, or in places open to the public, must provide written notice to the president of the municipal chamber with territorial jurisdiction over the area at least two working days prior to the event.[5]
>
> . . .
>
> The authorities may stop meetings, rallies, demonstrations, or parades being held in public places, or in places open to the public, only when they are contrary to law or morality, or when they seriously disrupt order, public tranquility, [or] the free exercise of individual rights, or violate the provisions of article 1(2) of Decree-Law No. 406 of August 29, 1974.[6]

---

[1] CONSTITUIÇÃO DA REPÚBLICA PORTUGUESA (VII REVISÃO CONSTITUCIONAL, 2005), art. 45(1), http://www. parlamento.pt/Legislacao/Paginas/ConstituicaoRepublicaPortuguesa.aspx.

[2] *Id.* art. 45(2).

[3] Decreto-Lei No. 406/74, de 29 de Agosto, art. 1(1), https://dre.pt/application/dir/pdf1sdip/1974/08/20101/00020003.pdf.

[4] *Id.* art. 1(2).

[5] Decreto-Lei No. 406/74, de 29 de Agosto, *as amended by* Lei Orgânica No. 1/2011, de 30 de Novembro, art. 2(1), http://www.pgdlisboa.pt/leis/lei_mostra_articulado.php?artigo_id=1568A0002&nid=1568&tabela=leis&pagina=1&ficha=1&nversao.

[6] Decreto-Lei No. 406/74, art. 5.

Spain

Graciela Rodriguez-Ferrand
Senior Foreign Law Specialist

The Spanish Constitution recognizes the right to peaceful, unarmed assembly without prior authorization.[1] In the event of meetings and demonstrations in public places, however, prior notification must be given to the authorities, who may ban such meetings only when there are well-founded grounds to expect a breach of public order, involving danger to persons or property.[2]

The Constitutional Court, in interpreting this provision, has observed that any demonstration in a public transit area that hinders or obstructs the normal patterns of social and community life, such as by impeding traffic flow, may be deemed to endanger the integrity of persons or property.[3] However, in determining whether to restrict such a demonstration, the authorities must apply the principle of proportionality. That principle requires consideration of whether the restriction would achieve a legitimate goal, whether that goal could be achieved by less restrictive means, and whether the costs of the restriction outweigh its benefits.[4] The Constitutional Court has also reiterated in several decisions that the behavior of the participants and their reaction to the police force's presence must be considered before any restriction or sanction is imposed.[5]

In implementing the constitutional right to peaceful unarmed assembly, Organic Law 9/1983 Regulating the Right of Assembly provides that no meeting requires previous authorization[6] unless it is being held in a place of "public transit", in which case the organizers of such a meeting or march must notify government authorities in writing a minimum of ten and a maximum of thirty days prior to the event.[7]

Holding a march or protest without the requisite prior notification makes its organizers or leaders liable to administrative sanctions, according to the Organic Law on Public Safety.[8] However,

---

[1] CONSTITUCIÓN ESPANOLA [C.E.] [SPANISH CONSTITUTION] art. 21(1), BOLETÍN OFICIAL DEL ESTADO [B.O.E.], Dec. 29, 1978, https://www.boe.es/legislacion/documentos/ConstitucionCASTELLANO.pdf.

[2] *Id.* art. 21(2).

[3] Sentencia Tribunal Constitucional STC 66/1995, May 8, 1995, available on the Constitutional Court website, *at* http://hj.tribunalconstitucional.es/HJ/es/Resolucion/Show/2920.

[4] *Id.*

[5] *Id.*

[6] Ley Orgánica 9/1983, Reguladora del Derecho de Reunión [Law 9/1983 Regulating the Right of Assembly] art. 3, B.O.E., July 18, 1983, http://boe.es/buscar/act.php?id=BOE-A-1983-19946.

[7] *Id.* art. 8, para. 1.

[8] Ley Orgánica 1/1992 de Seguridad Ciudadana [Organic Law on Public Safety] art. 23(c), B.O.E., Feb. 1, 1992, https://www.boe.es/buscar/act.php?id=BOE-A-1992-4252.

such sanctions only apply to an event's organizers or leaders, not to the participants, because participants may not be aware of the lack of compliance with the notification requirement.[9]

Organic Law 9/1983 provides that government authorities may suspend or break up meetings or marches under the following conditions:

a) When they are considered illegal according to criminal law.

b) When they create public disturbances, putting people or property at risk.

c) When participants wear paramilitary uniforms.[10]

The Penal Code prohibits assemblies or demonstrations whose purpose is the perpetration of a crime or at which participants carry weapons, explosives, or blunt or otherwise dangerous objects.[11]

---

[9] Miguel Ángel Presno Linera, *El Derecho de Reunión y Manifestación Resumido para Juristas y no Juristas, Ministros del Interior Incluidos* [*The Right of Assembly and Protests Summarized for Jurists and Nonjurists, Including Ministers of the Interior*], ¿HAY DERECHO? (Oct. 3, 2012), http://hayderecho.com/2012/10/03/el-derecho-de-reunion-y-manifestacion-resumido-para-juristas-y-no-juristas-ministros-del-interior-incluidos/.

[10] Ley Orgánica 9/1983, art. 5.

[11] CÓDIGO PENAL [PENAL CODE] art. 513, B.O.E., Nov. 24, 1995, https://www.boe.es/buscar/act.php?id=BOE-A-1995-25444.

Sweden

Elin Hofverberg
Foreign Law Research Consultant

I. Right of Peaceful Assembly

The rights of peaceful assembly, to protest, and to hold religious meetings are protected by the Swedish Constitution.[1] These rights may only be limited by legislation.[2] In addition, Sweden has adopted the European Convention on Human Rights, and is therefore bound by judgments construing the Convention that relate to peaceful assembly.[3]

Under Sweden's Constitution, limits on the personal freedoms mentioned above may only be imposed if the measure taken meets objectives acceptable in a democratic society. A limitation may never exceed what is necessary or go so far as to "constitute a threat to the formation of opinions or one of the foundations of democracy."[4] In addition, a limitation may not be based solely on the "political, religious or other similar opinion" of an individual.[5]

The right of assembly and the right to protest may only be limited to the extent necessary to protect peace and security during the assembly, for traffic reasons, for national security reasons, or to prevent disease.[6] The right of association can be limited but only for military groups and groups whose activities constitute "persecution of another group based on its ethnic origin, skin color or other similar circumstance."[7] The constitutional limits on the right of assembly are also reiterated in the Public Order Act.[8] The public broadcasting of pornography is specifically prohibited.[9] In addition, the government may designate certain geographic areas as off limits to protests if done to protect national security.[10]

---

[1] REGERINGSFORMEN [RF] [CONSTITUTION] ch. 2:1 item 3, ch. 2:4, ch. 2:6.

[2] *Id.* ch. 2:20.

[3] LAG OM DEN EUROPEISKA KONVENTIONEN ANGÅENDE SKYDD FOR DE MÄNSKLIGA RÄTTIGHETERNA OCH DE GRUNDLÄGGANDE FRIHETERNA [ACT ON THE EUROPEAN CONVENTION ON THE PROTECTION FOR THE HUMAN RIGHTS AND FUNDAMENTAL FREEDOMS] (Svensk författningssamling [SFS] 1994:1219). For a discussion of the Convention, see the European Court of Human Rights survey, *supra*.

[4] RF ch. 2:21.

[5] *Id.* (translation by author).

[6] *Id.* ch. 2:24 para. 1.

[7] *Id.* ch. 2:24 para. 2 (translation by author).

[8] ORDNINGSLAGEN (SFS 1993:1617) 2:10.

[9] *Id.* ch. 2:14.

[10] *Id.* ch. 2:15, para. 1.

II. Notification or Police Authorization for Peaceful Assemblies

Public assemblies are regulated in the Public Order Act.[11] Those who organize assemblies must either give notice in advance or obtain police authorization, depending on the type of event.

A very limited number of public assemblies are exempt from the authorization requirement and instead only require advance notice to the police a week prior to the event. These are cinematic or musical performances that are of no threat to the safety of the attendees and would not cause disruption to traffic.[12] An application for authorization to hold a public assembly must be submitted in all other cases and should be submitted to the police one week prior to the meeting, if possible.[13] Both applications and notifications should include "information on the organizers, the time and place of the assembly, the type of assembly, and its main design as well as the security measure that the organizers are planning."[14] An application for authorization needs to be in writing whereas a notification can be made either in writing or orally.[15]

The police may terminate or cancel an authorized or unauthorized public assembly if there is a "considerable risk of danger to those attending or a serious disturbance of traffic."[16] Such actions can only be taken, however, if less invasive and restrictive actions have proven unsuccessful.[17] The police may also deny applications for types of public assemblies that previously resulted in violence or danger that warranted the cancellation or termination of the event.[18] A decision by the police in relation to a public assembly can be appealed to the administrative courts.[19]

The approval of a protest entitles protestors to police protection. An unauthorized public assembly receives no planned police protection but the fact that it is unauthorized does not in and of itself constitute grounds for termination of the assembly.[20] A further reason, as outlined above, must also be present.

---

[11] *Id.* ch. 2:4, ch. 2:6.

[12] *See id.* ch. 2:4 para. 2 (permitting cinematic and other musical performances to be held in public without prior permission if there is no threat to the safety of the attendees).

[13] *Id.* ch. 2:6.

[14] *Id.* ch. 2:7 (translation by author).

[15] *Id.* ch. 2:6.

[16] *Id.* ch. 2:23 item 1 (translation by author).

[17] *Id.* ch. 2:24.

[18] *Id.* ch. 2:25.

[19] *Id.* ch. 2:28.

[20] *See* Proposition [Prop.] 1992/93:210 [Government Bill] at 79 & 262, http://www.riksdagen.se/sv/Dokument-Lagar/Forslag/Propositioner-och-skrivelser/om-ny-ordningslag-mm_GG03210/?text=true. However, the organizers of an unauthorized assembly can be punished under 2:29 ORDNINGSLAGEN for failure to secure prior authorization.

III. Court Cases

Appeals of decisions to grant or deny authorization for a demonstration are filed with the administrative courts. The Justitieombudsmän (Parliamentary Ombudsmen) also investigate the exercise of public authority and issues critiques against police handling of authorizations or denials for public assemblies, and police protection of such assemblies.[21] The Parliamentary Ombudsmen can investigate following a complaint or on their own initiative.[22]

The Parliamentary Ombudsmen have issued critiques against the police for busing protestors to another location,[23] for terminating a demonstration without legal cause,[24] and for terminating an authorized protest without first trying to secure the protest by removing violent individuals from an unauthorized counterdemonstration.[25] The Parliamentary Ombudsmen have also criticized local police guidelines where the number of protests in a given area by a given organization was limited to six per year.[26]

---

[21] *See* ACT WITH INSTRUCTIONS FOR THE PARLIAMENTARY OMBUDSMEN [LAG MED INSTRUKTION FÖR RIKSDAGENS OMBUDSMÄN] arts. 2 & 3 (SFS 1986:765), http://www.jo.se/en/About-JO/Legal-basis/Instructions/ (in English).

[22] *Id.* arts. 5, 5a, 6.

[23] Justitieombudsman [JO] Critique 2002-08-22, No. 3489-2001, Claes Eklundh; JO Critique 2003-04-23, No. 1508-2002, Claes Eklundh.

[24] JO Critique 2008-04-10, No. 2128-2006, Mats Melin.

[25] JO Critique 2010-12-12, Nos. 597-2006, 598-2006, 632-2006, and 776-2006, Mats Melin.

[26] JO:S ÄMBETSBERÄTTELSE [JO'S ANNUAL OFFICIAL REPORT] 1982/83 at 95.

United Kingdom

Clare Feikert-Ahalt
Senior Foreign Law Specialist

I. Introduction

The United Kingdom's Human Rights Act 1998 provides that every person in the UK has a number of fundamental rights and freedoms, and incorporates the European Convention on Human Rights into the domestic law of the UK.[1] These include the right to freedom of expression and the right to assemble peacefully and associate with others.[2] Restrictions may only be placed on this right if prescribed by law and necessary in a democratic society.[3] The Act does not prevent the police, armed forces, or administrators of the state from imposing lawful restrictions on the exercise of peaceful assembly and freedom of association.[4]

II. Notices for Public Processions and Assemblies

Limits to public processions and assemblies have been imposed by the Public Order Act 1986.[5] This Act provides that the police should be given notice of a public procession in writing at least six days prior to the procession.[6] There are exceptions to this notification requirement, including where the procession is one that is commonly or customarily held, and for funeral processions organized by a funeral director.[7]

The Public Order Act 1986 also allows the police to impose conditions on both public processions and public assemblies if they believe serious public disorder, property damage, or disruption will occur, or if the purpose of the procession is to intimidate others.[8] The conditions imposed must be necessary to prevent the issue of concern, and may include restrictions on the

---

[1] Human Rights Act 1998, c. 42, sch. 1, http://www.legislation.gov.uk/ukpga/1998/42/schedule/1.

[2] *Id.* arts. 10(1) & 11(1).

[3] *Id.* arts. 10(2) & 11(2). Any restrictions must be necessary in a democratic society and "in the interests of national security or public safety, for the prevention of disorder or crime, for the protection of health or morals or for the protection of the rights and freedoms of others." *Id.* art. 11(2). The Act further provides that there must be no discrimination in the operation of these rights and freedoms on any grounds, including sex, race, religion, or political views. *Id.* art. 14. More detailed information on the rights provided by the European Convention on Human Rights, which governs the rights of people to assemble, is provided in the European Union survey.

[4] *Id.*

[5] "Public assembly" is defined in the Act as an assembly of twenty or more people in a public place that is "wholly or partly open to the air." The term "public procession" means a procession in a public place. Public Order Act 1986, c. 64, § 16, http://www.legislation.gov.uk/ukpga/1986/64.

[6] *Id.* § 11.

[7] *Id.* § 11(2).

[8] *Id.* § 14.

route of processions or prohibitions on entering public places.[9] Conditions on public assemblies can include restrictions on location, the number of people allowed in attendance, or duration.[10] These conditions may be placed in advance of the procession or assembly, or at the time of it. Failing to comply with any conditions is a criminal offense punishable by up to three months' imprisonment and/or a fine.

III. Prohibiting Public Processions and Assemblies

Public processions may be prohibited if the chief of police believes that imposing the conditions discussed above will not be sufficient to prevent public disorder.[11] The process for prohibiting a procession is through the district council, upon the application of the chief of police. The prohibition must be approved by the Secretary of State, who then issues a procession prohibition order.

There are special rules regulating activities outside of Parliament in London, where assemblies and processions are commonly held. The Police Reform and Social Responsibility Act 2011 controls the activities that may occur in Parliament Square Garden and on its adjacent sidewalks. The Act prohibits the use of amplifiers and the use of tents or structures designed to allow people to sleep or stay in that area.[12]

IV. Cases

In the case of *Jukes v. Director of Public Prosecutions*, the divisional court held that leaving a route agreed to by demonstrators in order to join another demonstration is an offense if, at the time of leaving, the protesters were still participants of the first demonstration to which the conditions applied.[13]

---

[9] *Id.* § 12(2).

[10] *Id.* § 14(1).

[11] *Id.* § 13.

[12] Police Reform and Social Responsibility Act 2011, c. 13, pt. 3, http://www.legislation.gov.uk/ukpga/2011/13/contents/enacted.

[13] Jukes v. Director of Public Prosecutions, (2013) 177 JP 212, [2013] EWHC 195 (Admin), *cited in* BLACKSTONE'S CRIMINAL JUSTICE 2014 (Rt. Hon. Sir Anthony Hooper et al. eds. 2014), ¶ B11.112.

United States

Andrew M. Winston
Legal Reference Librarian

The First Amendment to the United States Constitution prohibits the United States Congress from enacting legislation that would abridge the right of the people to assemble peaceably.[1] The Fourteenth Amendment to the United States Constitution makes this prohibition applicable to state governments.[2]

The Supreme Court of the United States has held that the First Amendment protects the right to conduct a peaceful public assembly.[3] The right to assemble is not, however, absolute. Government officials cannot simply prohibit a public assembly in their own discretion,[4] but the government can impose restrictions on the time, place, and manner of peaceful assembly, provided that constitutional safeguards are met.[5] Time, place, and manner restrictions are permissible so long as they "are justified without reference to the content of the regulated speech, . . . are narrowly tailored to serve a significant governmental interest, and . . . leave open ample alternative channels for communication of the information."[6]

Such time, place, and manner restrictions can take the form of requirements to obtain a permit for an assembly.[7] The Supreme Court has held that it is constitutionally permissible for the government to require that a permit for an assembly be obtained in advance.[8] The government

---

[1] The First Amendment states that "*Congress shall make no law* respecting an establishment of religion, or prohibiting the free exercise thereof; or *abridging* the freedom of speech, or of the press; or *the right of the people peaceably to assemble*, and to petition the Government for a redress of grievances." U.S. CONST. AMEND. I (emphasis added), *available at* http://www.archives.gov/exhibits/charters/bill_of_rights_transcript.html.

[2] U.S. CONST. AMEND. XIV, § 1, *available at* http://www.archives.gov/exhibits/charters/constitution_amendments_11-27.html; *see* Hague v. C.I.O., 307 U.S. 496, 512 (1939), *available at* https://supreme.justia.com/cases/federal/us/307/496/case.html. In addition to the protections afforded by the United States Constitution, nearly all of the fifty states include protections for the right of assembly in their state constitutions. *See* the state constitutions accessible through the Law Library of Congress' Guide to Law Online. *Guide to Law Online: U.S. States & Territories*, LAW LIBR. OF CONG., http://www.loc.gov/law/help/guide/states.php (last visited Sept. 23, 2014).

[3] *Hague*, 307 U.S. 496.

[4] Shuttlesworth v. City of Birmingham, 394 U.S. 147, 150–51 (1969), *available at* https://supreme.justia.com/cases/federal/us/394/147/case.html.

[5] Ward v. Rock Against Racism, 491 U.S. 781, 791 (1989) (quoting Clark v. Cmty. For Creative Non-Violence, 468 U.S. 288, 293 (1984)) (internal citations omitted), *available at* https://supreme.justia.com/cases/federal/us/491/781/.

[6] *Id.*

[7] Thomas v. Chi. Park Dist., 534 U.S. 316, 322 (2002), *available at* https://supreme.justia.com/cases/federal/us/534/316/case.html.

[8] Cox v. New Hampshire, 312 U.S. 569, 575–76 (1941), *available at* https://supreme.justia.com/cases/federal/us/312/569/case.html.

can also make special regulations that impose additional requirements for assemblies that take place near major public events.[9]

In the United States, the organizer of a public assembly must typically apply for and obtain a permit in advance from the local police department or other local governmental body.[10] Applications for permits usually require, at a minimum, information about the specific date, time, and location of the proposed assembly, and may require a great deal more information.[11] Localities can, within the boundaries established by Supreme Court decisions interpreting the First Amendment right to assemble peaceably, impose additional requirements for permit applications, such as information about the organizer of the assembly and specific details about how the assembly is to be conducted.[12]

The First Amendment does not provide the right to conduct an assembly at which there is a clear and present danger of riot, disorder, or interference with traffic on public streets, or other immediate threat to public safety or order.[13] Statutes that prohibit people from assembling and using force or violence to accomplish unlawful purposes are permissible under the First Amendment.[14]

---

[9] Tabatha Abu El-Haj, *The Neglected Right of Assembly*, 56 UCLA L. REV. 543, 551–52 (2009), http://uclalaw review.org/pdf/56-3-1.pdf (discussing temporary restrictions in the context of protests at political conventions and international conferences, such as requirements that protestors gather in specified areas and that they apply for permits six months in advance).

[10] *Id.* at 548 (describing the results of the author's survey of assembly permit requirements in twenty US cities).

[11] *Id.* at 548–49.

[12] For example, in Chicago, Illinois, an applicant for a permit for a public assembly must indicate (among other things) the date, time, and location of the proposed assembly; the name, address, and on-site manager of and twenty-four-hour contact information for the event organizer; and the estimated number of attendees and the basis for that estimate. Chicago Dep't of Transp., Notification of Public Assembly, http://www.cityofchicago.org/dam/city/depts/cdot/permit/Applications/Public_Assembly_Notification.pdf (last visited Sept. 19, 2014). In Los Angeles, California, an applicant for a permit must provide information about (among other things) the date, time, and location of the proposed assembly; the name, address, and telephone number of the sponsoring organization and an official of that organization; and a description of how the event is to be conducted, including public notification plans. *Special Event Permits Unit and Permit Application Information*, LOS ANGELES POLICE DEPARTMENT http://www.lapdonline.org/search_results/content_basic_view/6521 (last visited Sept. 19, 2014).

[13] Jones v. Parmley, 465 F.3d 46, 56–57 (2d Cir. 2006), *available at* http://law.justia.com/cases/federal/appellate-courts/F3/465/46/544540/.

[14] Cole v. Arkansas, 338 U.S. 345 (1949), *available at* https://supreme.justia.com/cases/federal/us/338/345/case.html.